JIGGLE YOUR HEART AND TICKLE YOUR SOUL

The uses of joy and laughter in attaining health and happiness

By Anne Bryan Smollin, CSJ, PhD

For information about ordering more copies of this book, write:

Counseling for Laity
40 North Main Ave.
Albany, New York 12203

First Printing, October 1994
Second Printing, November 1994
Third Printing, December 1994
Fourth Printing, February 1995
Fifth Printing, April 1995
Sixth Printing, July 1995
Seventh Printing, November 1995

Cover design by James Breig and
Donna Wait Lesson

Publisher: Canticle Press
371 Watervliet-Shaker Rd.
Latham, NY 12110-4741

Library of Congress Catalog Card Number: 94-80148
ISBN: 0-9641725-2-6

DEDICATION
To my Mom, Irma,
and to my sister, Kay,
the wind beneath my wings

BIBLIOGRAPHY

Chopra, Deepak. AGELESS BODY, TIMELESS MIND. New York: Harmony Books, 1993.

Cousins, Norman. ANATOMY OF AN ILLNESS. New York: W. W. Norton & Co., 1979.

Frankl, Victor E. MAN'S SEARCH FOR MEANING. New York: Simon & Schuster, 1963.

Johnson, Barbara. SPLASHES OF JOY IN THE CESSPOOLS OF LIFE. Dallas: Word Publishing, 1992.

Klein, Allen. THE HEALING POWER OF HUMOR Los Angeles: Jeremy P. Tarcher, Inc., 1989.

Siegel, Bernie. LOVE, MEDICINE AND MIRACLES. New York: Harper & Row, 1986.

Swindoll, Charles R. LAUGH AGAIN. Dallas: Word Publishing, 1991.

TABLE OF CONTENTS

INTRODUCTION

This book is the result of a lot of things: some people encouraging me to write it; other people challenging me to finish it; workshops and lectures I've given on this topic; and even messages that have hit me along the way.

One day that was more hectic than most provided the final shove that made me take the time to complete this volume. I had several client appointments; and sandwiched in between them were two workshops and a dinner keynote address. The day before had been even more pressured. So, when I jumped in my car after having seen five clients and given a workshop to a hospice group on "Wellness and Humor," I began feeling very tired.

Trying to ignore this feeling because I still had to see one more client and then give the dinner address, I steered my car onto the New York State Thruway and began talking out loud to myself. I asked myself why I was working so hard and why I was accepting more speaking commitments. I began to talk about all the unfinished projects I had not gotten to. Then I engaged God in my conversation: "God, why am I doing all of this? What should I do and what should I let go of? You know, God, I do enjoy working, and I love all the lectures I give. But I can't keep up this pace much longer. And what about that book? Should I finish it or should I just forget the whole thing? God, if only You would help. If only You could send me a sign then I would know what I really should be doing."

As I said those words, I looked at the truck in front

of me. The back panel of the truck read: G.O.D. Call 1-800-DIAL-GOD

I got hysterical. I was laughing so loud that I thought if anyone looked at me, they would certainly question my mental health status. The "Guaranteed Overnight Delivery" truck had delivered my answer, and I began to put my energies into completing this book.

A project like this does not happen alone. It is the result of many colleagues talking together and challenging one another. It comes because people share moments of life with each other. And those life-giving moments are filled with humor, joy and laughter. Some are even filled with tears. Books are summaries of experiences and re-corded memories of meaningful events and situations. This one is no different. Supportive friends offered healthy, welcomed nudges. My friends are always there. They are supportive and challenging and life-giving. Patti and Janet truly touch my soul. I belong to the religious community of the Sisters of St. Joseph and always feel at home. I work in a warm, caring environment with people who believe in life and living. A special thanks to Jim Breig and Kathy Rooke for their editing help.

In addition, the belief and pride of my mother and sister have always been a strength, encouraging me to believe this could be a possibility.

While I can't forget the G.O.D. truck that carried a very direct message, I believe in my God (the One not related to the truck) Who graces me daily.

This book belongs to all of them. Thanks. Stay happy. Laugh much. And believe in yourself.

Anne

Chapter One

❧

ME AND THE ULTIMATE WARRIOR

There's nothing like a good laugh. It tickles our very souls. Laughter is an activity of the heart. We scrunch our souls with negativity and a lack of enthusiasm. Laughter smoothes them out. Laughter makes a noise so others can hear our feelings.

Joy is a state of mind. It really is an attitude which keeps us healthy. We are all born with a sense of humor, but it is a gift we must develop as we age. This process does not end until death. The pay-off for developing a sense of humor is that we simultaneously opt for health and wellness.

That's what this book is all about. It's about joy and laughter and humor. It's about alternatives to help us live happier lives and help those around us enjoy us even more. It's about filling our hearts with life. It's about wrinkling our faces with smiles and not drying up our souls like prunes.

It's time we looked for smiles and joy and laughter and happiness. No one needs to look for sadness; it has a strange way of hitting us right in the face. Everyone has a horror story to tell or a crisis to relate.

Maybe we get so bogged down in our tough times that we forget there's always another side we can look at. Or perhaps it's fear that no one will think we're important enough or think we need them that leads us to hold on to our heavy, sad, depressing stories.

Joy can lighten our environment. Joy frees us to breathe more easily and see things more clearly. Joy lets oxygen into our blood and into our brains. When that happens, we begin to think differently. We can be healthier, more relaxed people. The Jesuit theologian DeChardin wrote, "Joy is the most infallible sign of the presence of God." Perhaps we can begin to see this presence of God in one another; if we did, then we would start to treat each other in a kinder, more thoughtful, more respectful way.

And it all starts with "you" — the person you look at in the mirror! Because joy is really not "doing"; it's really more like "being."

Many people have not learned the importance of taking care of themselves. We give others endless hours of our time. We begin to stutter when we have to say "no." However, if we don't take care of ourselves, we can never begin truly to pay attention to or minister to anyone else.

Recently, I was on an airplane. As is the case for many persons who travel often, I tend not to listen to the flight attendant as she instructs the passengers. The message is always the same, no matter what airline you're on. This time, however, I became distracted when I heard the flight attendant say: "And when the oxygen mask drops down, put it over your own face before you put it over the face of your child."

As she said those words, I found myself watching a mother two seats in front of me play with her little child. I began thinking about what I would do if that child were mine. I would want to protect the child and be sure the child was safe. That would be my first instinct. I would want to put the oxygen over the child's face first — and then attend to myself.

I started to picture what would happen in the jet if that scene became a reality. The cabin pressure would change so immediately that if I did not place the oxygen mask over my own face first, I would not be able to think clearly and would not have the ability to attend to the child.

Oh, the importance of taking care of ourselves! This in no way implies that we become self-centered or selfish. Rather, it means that if we do not have a respect for ourselves and a healthy sense of self-importance, then it is nearly impossible for us to develop a respect and healthy sense of importance for others.

One way to begin to take care of ourselves is to laugh. If you think about it, humor is a pretty cheap remedy. It costs nothing, and the results are fantastic. We don't need to go to a physician and seek a prescription. All we need to do is to change some negative perceptions and attitudes. And relax.

If only it were that easy! Still, we are going to use up energy one way or another, so why not make the choice that has positive pay-offs?

Humor releases the same endorphins that jogging does, so we get a natural high without the purchase of new running shoes and clothing. Perhaps the most consoling piece of information is that we don't have to hurt our knees or ankles or jar any muscles or major organs to enjoy this surge of positive feeling.

Humor heals and relaxes. It renews the joy that gets hammered out of us by life's daily shocks. Humor gives us power. We often cannot control situations or events, but we can control our response to them. When we choose humor as our response instead of discouragement or despair, we claim power.

The image we have of ourselves and the image others perceive are so important. How we look, how we dress, our facial expressions, how others hear our message, our eye contact — all of those create our image. Sometimes, we think, "Oh, she's in a good mood," just because the person has a smile on her face. Or we might decide, "This is not a good time to bring this item up to him," because of the expression on his face.

The examples of how we make judgments on our observations are countless. Recently, I gave a keynote address for a Catholic School Superintendents' Day. The day began with Mass. The woman who organized the service stood behind the podium on the altar and began giving the instructions: "Please stand and greet the celebrant, and sing the opening song, 'I've got that joy, joy, joy, joy down in my heart.'"

As she spoke, she stared at the group with a face that would have stopped the Energizer Bunny. I thought of how little joy was reflected in her face. It said anything but happiness to me. Yes, I judged on nonverbals. However, we must remember that so often that is our only source of information.

One time when I was on a business trip to Hawaii, everyone in the airport seemed to know this tall, good-looking, very muscular gentleman. He was surrounded by people asking for his autograph. I kept trying to find out who he was and finally decided to be direct. I said to him, "Everyone else seems to know who you are. But I don't. Who are you?" He responded, "I'm the Ultimate Warrior!" I quickly said, "I still don't know who you are!" He told me he was the World Wrestling Federation champion. I could have guessed he was a wrestler. He neck was as thick as a tree trunk! We had a lovely conversation about kids today, schools, families and values, among other things.

The day I returned home from that trip, I spoke at a high school to almost 700 students. I began wondering how to get their attention. These students had no idea who I was or why they should stop talking to their friends to listen to someone they had never seen before. I decided that if I told them the story of the Ultimate Warrior, I would become an instant hero.

When I finished my story, one kid yelled, "You met the Ultimate Warrior?" I said, "Yes." He continued, "What did he look like?" I responded, "Just like us." Suspiciously, he said, "No, he doesn't." I said, "Yes, he does." He insisted, "No, he doesn't." I said, "Yes, he does."

Then another student yelled, "What did he sound like?" I said, "Just like us." Skeptically, he said, "No, he doesn't." I said, "Yes, he does." He maintained, "No, he doesn't." I said, "Yes, he does."

I couldn't figure out why the students doubted that

I had really met the Ultimate Warrior. In fact, I was beginning to wonder if I really had. The following Sunday, I was at my mother's home for dinner. I knew that wrestling was on TV, so I began to zap through the channels to find the right program. Anyone who watches wrestling regularly would know that I didn't succeed because each wrestler appears only every three or four weeks. So it took me three Sundays to see the Ultimate Warrior. (I received a wonderful education during those three weeks, however. I met The Undertaker and his assistant, Pall Bearer; Tugboat; The Million Dollar Man; The Bushwhackers; and others.)

Finally, on the television screen appeared the Ultimate Warrior. No wonder the kids had questioned my description of him as looking and sounding like the rest of us. The man on the TV had paint all over his face, and he was screaming into the television: "My warriors will come and get you." That wasn't the man I had met at the airport.

I wonder how often we see others as the Ultimate Warrior, and how often others see us as the Ultimate Warrior. I met the real person at the airport; he is not the painted wrestler I saw on the screen. That one is an actor. If we stand in front of others, or if we work with some people, or if we live with someone, and if all we see is the Ultimate Warrior and never take the time to know the real person, we will never have the joy of encountering the person who is in front of us. If others see us only as the Ultimate Warrior and never get to know the true person we are, a moment of joy (or many moments of positive energy) may be lost forever.

Check yourself in the mirror. How much war paint do you wear? Do you look like you would more eagerly hand out chokeholds than hugs?

Chapter Two

❧

THE 70-MPH EXPLOSION

W hat happens to us that robs us of our sense of humor?

What drains us so that we are willing to let go of such a life-giving grace?

Research indicates that an infant laughs when she is ten weeks old. At sixteen weeks, an infant laughs almost every hour. When a child is four years old, he laughs every four minutes — unless we interfere with the child experiencing joy!

It's a fact: When we laugh more and when we have a sense of humor, we are more creative thinkers and healthier people.

A good laugh releases mental and physical tension in our bodies. Our whole body benefits when we laugh. Our temperature goes up at least one degree. The larynx and glottis begin to rock. Air rises along the windpipe and bangs against the trachea. Laughter then explodes out of our bodies at almost 70 miles an hour. For all those people who are worried about getting old and slowing down, remember that we can still do something at 70 miles an hour all our lives!

Laugher and joy have healing aspects. Four ways to heal ourselves are by laughing, crying, yawning and having sex. "Having sex" doesn't mean having sexual intercourse. We are all sexual people. We are born that way. All of us know what happens to a baby if he is not held or touched: He dies. We must remember that we never outgrow the need to be touched or held. How many times can you remember being hurt or feeling despair and then having someone just hug you or put an arm around you? No words of consolation or understanding can ever match that gesture!

Laughter keeps us open to the possibilities and options that are available. So often, we let our attitudes or anxieties lead us to the point of not being able to see the whole picture. We get stuck in our own "stuckness." We walk around with blinders on, seeing only from a narrow point of view. As a result, everything gets heavy and black and bleak. Sadness and depression may overcome us.

What a wonderful gift when someone can free us from the feelings that weigh us down and help us learn to laugh, smile and see some healthy options. It's happened to all of us: We are in a situation where the tension is so thick that you can hardly breathe. Then someone says something, and everyone laughs. You know how it feels. Your body relaxes, and the tension in your neck and back goes away.

Humor helps us to see through things. It offers us bifocals even when we don't think we need to wear glasses. It keeps things in perspective. Humor sometimes even creates a three-dimensional focus for us. As a result, our perceptions and our attitudes can be altered. Then we can find healthier and new ways to approach a situation.

So often, what blocks us from seeing and experiencing humor and joy is our attitude. We hold on to negative thoughts and situations that have occurred in our life. They become the driving forces that determine our beliefs and thoughts and actions.

One bad experience, one rejection, one significant loss, one person saying something bad about us, someone not liking something we've done, not receiving the approval of a co-worker or friend — incidents like those become obsessions, and we measure everything by them.

They also become our "un-freedoms." They are nooses we tie around our own necks. They become our controllers, so we choke any joy from our perception and allow the negatives to block our pores.

Sometimes, it takes work to be able to see the joy and humor that exist right in front of us. Anthony DeMello told a wonderful story about a man who wanted desperately to win the lottery. He prayed, "Dear God, please let me win the lottery!" The next week, he prayed louder, "Dear God, please let me win the lottery. My family will be taken care of." Each week, he prayed a bit louder. Finally, about six months later, he was on his knees with his hands folded tightly, shouting: "Please God, let me win the lottery. My family needs so many things. Then they will be taken care of." From Heaven, he heard a booming voice: "It would be helpful if you bought a ticket."

That's what it's all about. We have to buy lottery tickets! We can't just assume that humor or joy will hit us in the face. We have to start to look for it the way a gold prospector looks for nuggets.

It's also important to address our own perceptions and attitudes. So many of us hold on to negative thoughts without even being aware of what those thoughts are doing to us. They act as shut-off valves in our lives, cutting off all life-giving thoughts. These negative thoughts block the oxygen flow to our brain; before long, we are emotionally comatose.

Since negative thinking clogs the brain, it is obvious that positive thinking unclogs it, allowing creativity and options to flow freely. We begin to find ourselves energized. Our stress level decreases, and our attitudes begin to be positive.

We must become aware of our perceptions, and of the fears and biases that shape those perceptions. Our own desires and wishes, at times, determine what we see (or want to see). Perhaps you have heard of the farmer who had only one dream: for his two sons to inherit the farm and to love it as much as he did. For one of his sons, that might happen, but the other wasn't sure. Daily, that son searched for an answer as to what he would do with his life. Should he stay and be a farmer, or should he go off and get involved in another line of work? One day, he ran across the farm, calling out to his father. Now he knew the answer; he knew he needed to leave the farm.

As he approached his father, he hurriedly told him that he had to leave the farm to go and preach Christ.

The father was rather puzzled at this announcement and asked how his son had reached his decision. The son said, "Oh, it was really easy. I was looking up at the clouds and I saw two letters — 'P.C.' That means 'Preach Christ.'" The father looked at his son and asked: "What makes you think it doesn't mean 'Pick Corn'?"

We are all like the farmer's son at times. We want something to be a certain way, so we put blinders on and limit our vision. The worst part is that some of us become so convinced we are right that we close our minds and seal our ears to any other alternatives. But humor and joy open our minds, ears and eyes to new possibilities and opportunities.

Chapter Three

&

WOBBLING ON THE TARMAC

W hen our attitudes are negative, we begin to perceive ourselves very negatively, and we let our self-esteem be determined by those dark thoughts.

A client of mine was always putting herself down. Nothing she ever did was right. She lived in Albany, New York, and was going to visit a friend in Fort Lauderdale, Florida. She had to fly from Albany and change planes in Philadelphia in order to get to Fort Lauderdale. Step one went fine, but in Philadelphia she somehow got back on the same plane she had just left. That jet took her to West Palm Beach, instead of Fort Lauderdale. Those two airports are about twenty minutes from each other. At her next session with me, all she could say was how dumb she was and how stupid she was and how no one else had ever made mistakes like hers.

I tried to get her to see that this was not a crisis, that she hadn't suffered anything drastic. She had simply ended up at another airport which was only twenty minutes from where she was supposed to be. She could not hear that. To her, no one ever could have made a mistake like hers!

During the session, I tried everything I had ever learned in school (and even things I did not learn in school) to get her off of this self-hatred. No luck! This went on for three sessions. It even got worse: I learned that once she had arrived at her friend's house in Fort Lauderdale, she had never left it because she was afraid she would not be able to find her way back. How our fears can control us!

At the third session, I tried to put some reality into this scene for her one more time. I said, "I fell off of a plane once!" There was no reaction, so I continued with my story. I was on my way to Muskegon, Michigan, and I was supposed to go from Albany to Pittsburgh and then on to Chicago. There, I would change planes and go to Muskegon. When I arrived in Pittsburgh, however, they announced that the plane was not going on to Chicago. We had to get off and make other arrangements.

By the time I arrived in Chicago, I had missed my connection to Muskegon. They then took us by bus to a tiny airport — the kind that has no people, only a few vending machines. There, I decided to call ahead and tell the person picking me up what time I would be arriving. I opened up my folder to get the number of the CEO of the hospital at which I was giving the workshop — only to find I did not have her home number, only the hospital number. I decided this was no problem because, surely, the hospital operator would be gracious enough to call her at home and relay the message.

I then opened up my wallet and found I had several bills but no coins. I decided I could call collect. The operator announced she had a collect call, but the woman answering the phone at the hospital quickly responded that she did not have the authority to accept it. I said, "It's no problem. I will pay you tomorrow." She said, "But I can't. I'll lose my job!" I hurriedly said, "No, you won't. The CEO is a friend of mine." She again reminded me that she didn't have the authority to accept this collect call. I pleaded, "But I'm stuck in an airport."

By this time, the operator decided to get involved. She said, "She's stuck in an airport. Can't you accept these charges? She said she'd pay you back tomorrow." The woman helplessly responded, "I hope I won't lose my job." The operator quickly stated, "You won't. The CEO is a friend of hers!" Only because the operator helped me did the woman at the hospital finally agree.

After relaying the time-of-arrival change, I sat down to read a novel. When it was finally time to depart, we were led to a small plane in the middle of the airfield. Small? It was the kind of plane you crawl into, the type that holds five-and-a-half people! There is no distinction between the passengers and the pilot in these small planes. Everyone is in first class!

As we were departing the plane in Muskegon, the lone person who tripled as pilot, steward and baggageman chatted with each of us. Pointing at the floor by the exit door, he said to me, "Don't catch your heel on that piece of aluminum." Anyone can guess what happened. It's called the "self-fulfilling prophecy." I caught my heel on the piece of aluminum and fell down the whole flight of stairs. As I tumbled, the thought that flashed through my mind wasn't: "How many bones am I going to break?" It was: "Don't ruin your outfit. It's the only one you have!"

I lay upside down on the stairs of the plane like a valise no one had claimed. When I got to my feet and leaned against the handrail, I turned to the gentleman behind me and told him I must have really clunked my head because I was so dizzy. I was rocking back and forth, unable to keep my balance, wondering if I had suffered a concussion. The man told me, politely, that I hadn't suffered anything more damaging than losing the heels to both my shoes. Then he scrambled under the plane to retrieve them. I was tottering back and forth because of my shoes. If anyone thinks that women's shoes become flat when the heels are removed, think again. Heel-less shoes become like boats. They pitch and roll — and I pitched and rolled with them.

I tiptoed from the middle of the field into the airport with the two busted heels clutched in the palm of my hand. Inside, I was warmly greeted by the CEO. She told me we were going to dinner at a restaurant of a friend of hers and that it didn't matter what time it was. I held my hand out to show her my two heels. She asked, "What are they?" I replied, "My heels. I fell off the plane!" Then we laughed loudly.

Now, I don't think I am stupid because I fell off the plane. I've done smarter things than that in my life, but I'm not dumb because I fell off a plane. You see, it's all in our attitudes and in what we tell ourselves about ourselves.

Our attitudes are learned things. If we become

aware that we are holding on to negative attitudes, isn't it wonderful to know we have the power to change them? We never have to hold on to anything that drags us down or ties a noose around our neck. We can repair our attitudes as quickly as a cobbler can fix a pair of heel-less shoes.

Chapter Four

THE WORRY CHAIR

Our parents have helped us know who we are. They gave us positive messages, and they gave us negative messages. Perhaps you grew up in a home environment where you were always told that you were dumb and stupid and never did anything right. If that was the case, then maybe today you still believe all those things. But you don't have to.

My mother always told me not only that I could do anything but also that I would do it well. I still believe that. One needs only to look at my calendar to see that I still believe I can do anything — and everything! But just hearing positive messages doesn't assure us that we always make healthy choices. The marvelous poet e.e. cummings reminds us, "It takes COURAGE to grow up and turn out to be who you really are."

I once was handed a piece of paper that had only a quotation from Charles Swindoll, the author and lecturer, on it. It was titled "ATTITUDE." It is one of those wonderful messages we can read over and over again:

"The longer I live, the more I realize the impact of

attitude on life. Attitude, to me, is more important than facts. It is more important than the past, than education, than money, than circumstances, than failures, than successes, than what other people think or say or do. It is more important than appearance, giftedness or skill. It will make or break a company...a church...a home. The remarkable thing is we have a choice every day regarding the attitude we will embrace for that day. We cannot change our past....We cannot change the fact that people will act in a certain way. We cannot change the inevitable. The only thing we can do is play on the one string we have, and that is our attitude....I am convinced that life is 10 percent what happens to me and 90 percent how I react to it. And let it begin with me."

We should carry around with us an imaginary ruler that goes from one to ten and realize that everything that happens does not deserve to be rated as an eight, nine or ten. Sometimes, things deserve to get only the energy of a one, two or three. Then we would conserve a lot of our energy and anxiety. We would also cut down drastically on the stress level we so often allow to govern us.

Some people are born worriers. They worry about what happens if something doesn't work out right. They worry about what happens if it does work out right. They can even find some "what if's" and "if only's" and "maybe's" to worry about in between.

Worry can be controlled. It is false to believe we can remove all worry from our lives. The secret is deciding when to worry. This can be done by determining a specific time or a specific place to focus on what we need to worry over. Pick a chair in your house. Decide that the only time you will worry is when you are sitting in that chair. Then, when you find yourself getting anxious and your mind is beginning to race a hundred miles an hour, tell your body that you are not going to think about that until you are sitting in that chair. When you awake in the middle of the night and you can't fall back asleep, tell your body you are not going to think about whatever is bothering you until you are sitting in that chair. Then roll over and fall back to sleep.

However, you must give yourself time to sit in that chair and worry every day. At first, begin with no more than a half hour. Do that for one week. Watch the way your body begins to believe you and gives you the choice of deciding when you will think and worry about what you want. Eventually, you can cut the time down until you will need only about five minutes each day. However, it is essential that you give your body and your mind that five minutes each day. What a small price to pay for twenty-three hours and fifty-five minutes of worry-free time every day!

There is another secret to dealing with worry: Stay in touch with NOW. So much humor, joy and happiness go unnoticed because we lose touch with reality. We walk around and lose focus. We can't see the trees for the forest. Perhaps one of the secrets is learning to be present to the NOW. We live so much in the future and the past that we miss the present moment — and that is where all the energy is. All the power for each one of us is in the present moment.

There is a wonderful Greek legend about Mother

Earth and her son Antaeus, fathered by Zeus. Antaeus was a wrestler who was invincible while in contact with the earth. He finally was defeated by Hercules, who lifted him into the air! All of Antaeus' energy was in the present. As long as we keep ourselves in the reality of NOW, we, too, can be invincible.

Another trick for handling worry is to realize that our thoughts influence our emotions. If we are thinking of something that makes us smile, we feel good and happy. If we are thinking of something that frightens us, our feelings follow.

Try it yourself:

1. Think of something or someone you love. What do you feel?

2. Next, think of something or someone you dislike. Now what do you feel?

3. Finally, think again of something or someone you love or makes you smile.

You see, when we change our thoughts, our emotions quickly follow.

Milton wrote in "Paradise Lost": "The mind is its own place, and in itself can make heaven of Hell, a hell of Heaven." If only we could believe in the power each one of us has for ourself.

Our bodies are powerful things, too. Our muscles can do only two things: relax and contract. As we begin to control our own lives, we learn how to relax and how to enjoy our present moment. Then we learn quickly that the key to playfulness is a sense of humor. It's like magic. We create our good times and our sense of humor out of a frame of mind. This occurs when we find ourselves in situations that we enjoy and when we are in the company of people we enjoy being with. And those are choices we can make.

Mark Twain gave us another option for making our choices. He suggested that "you never put off till tomorrow what you can do the day after tomorrow."

Chapter Five

YOU ARE WHAT YOU CARRY

W e all have a tendency to hold on to things that destroy us and cause us to stay unhealthy. As a result, the heaviness of our burdens prevents us from enjoying laughter. We get caught up in negativity and depression. The world becomes dark and big. We see the world through blinders. Everything is perceived as black and white.

Letting go of our hurts and disappointments, and learning to forgive ourselves and others are conscious acts. Forgiving someone or ourselves is not a feeling. It is a choice. We must choose to forgive.

Some people hold on to hurts and spend their whole lives being unhappy and miserable. Unfortunately, everyone who touches shoulders with such people senses the negative reactions and unhappiness. Who wants to be around someone who is always unhappy, always negative, always complaining? Still, these people hold on to this negativity and get some mileage out of it.

All of us get something — some payoff — when we hold on to things that are unhealthy. The unfortunate part is that, meanwhile, life keeps passing us by, and we miss all the healthy moments — moments filled with fun and laughter and positive energy. We get "stuck" in pain. This pain suffocates and strangles us, and we find ourselves not opting for life.

Some people hold on to words that were said to them years before. Some have not spoken for years to a person they loved for a reason they cannot even recall. People stay angry at others for days or weeks or years. Who pays the price for that? Only the person who holds on to the anger.

There is a marvelous story about two monks who were walking down a road and noticed a young woman waiting to cross a stream. One of the monks, to the dismay of the other, went to the woman, picked her up, and carried her across the water. He set her down, and she went on her way. The two monks then continued their own journey. About a mile down the road, the monk who was aghast at his friend's action remarked, "We are celibate. We are not even supposed to look at a woman, let alone pick one up and carry her across a stream. How could you possibly do that?" The other monk replied, "I put that woman down a mile back. Are you still carrying her around with you?"

We waste so much energy on old baggage, old thoughts, old hurts, old disappointments — and sometimes even other people's old baggage, old thoughts, old hurts, old disappointments. Our physical bodies don't hold on to dead skin. Every month — every 28 days — we become new people. If only we could do the same psychologically. If only we could shed our old baggage, how healthy we would be.

I sometimes believe we work harder at living than we have to. We take 20,000 breaths a day. What are we choosing to breathe in? Negative things? Things that tie a hangman's knot around our throats? Or are we consciously putting our energy into taking in positive air? Life-giving, pure, healthy air? We have learned to put those who smoke in a room by themselves so none of us has to allow that secondary smoke into our lungs. Can't we do the same with thoughts that are killing us — thoughts that are killing our spirits?

Recently, someone sent me a note card with a scene titled "The Brush Dance." The card revealed that "The Brush Dance was a Yurok Indian healing ritual where being true to yourself meant giving your best to help a person in need. Being true to yourself was the one and only Yurok Indian law."

Perhaps the simplicity of that culture can teach us something. Being "true to yourself" implies that your priorities are in place. And while "self" is important, selflessness is a healthy part of self. No one of us truly knows how powerful and important we are or the true potential each one of us possesses. Think what could really happen if we did believe in ourselves and were aware of the strength and power we had.

In "The Compassionate Universe," there is a wonderful story that Eknath Easwarn, author of "The Compassionate Universe," shares with us:

"I will never forget the day I came home from school and told my grandmother what I had learned in geography class. In our small South Indian village, my grandmother was deeply respected and loved. I could not imagine anyone wiser, yet she had never been to school or learned to read, or even traveled more than a few miles from our village. So when she met me at the gate, as she did every day, and asked me what I had learned in school, I was a bit hesitant to tell her the subject of the day's lesson. Apparently it was something every schoolboy should know and accept without difficulty. To me it was a catastrophe.

"'Granny,' I began with considerable agitation, 'scientists have discovered that our village is nothing but an anthill compared with the sun.' As always, she listened carefully to everything I had to say. I told her about the vastness of outer space, the tremendous distances between planets, and the terrible smallness of the world that had up to then been my universe: our village, the nearby forest, the Blue Mountain on the horizon. 'My teacher says we are just insignificant specks in the universe, Granny. We don't matter at all.'

"Generally, my grandmother spoke very little, but her presence communicated a tremendous security. She said nothing now. Calmly, she opened the gate, put her hand on my shoulder, and walked inside with me.

"We sat down, and it was a while before she spoke. 'No one is insignificant, son,' she said finally. 'Have you ever looked at Hasti's eyes?' Hasti was one of the elephants that frequently served in our religious ceremonies and that I had been learning to ride. Hasti's eyes, like the eyes of all elephants, were tiny — ridiculously small, really, for an animal so huge. 'She has no idea how big she is,' Granny said, 'because she looks out at the world through such tiny eyes.'"

We all have the potential to be a Hasti! We, too, look out at the world through such tiny eyes. But in no way are we insignificant! I wonder what would happen if we believed that. I wonder what our eyes would see then. We do not know who we truly are, how wonderful we are and the full potential we all have because, like Hasti, we are looking out through our own tiny eyes.

We could all use some wide-eyed excitement.

Chapter Six

❧

LIFE IS A BALANCING ACT

W e need to learn the secret of caring for ourselves. It's an everyday responsibility. It involves keeping our life in balance. It's about learning to make choices that keep us in touch with the core of who we are. It's knowing our own priorities.

There is a wonderful story about God appearing to a man in a dream. He told the man that a monk would walk past him at noontime the next day and that he would be carrying a stone. If the monk gave the man the stone, he would become the richest person in the world because the stone was a huge diamond.

When the man awoke, he couldn't wait to see if a monk would be passing by. Sure enough! At noon, a monk walked toward him and in his hand was a large satchel. The monk stopped and pulled out of the bag a diamond the size of a person's head! He told the man that he had found it in the forest. Then he gave it to the man. The man took the stone and ran home. He kept looking at it — and that kept reminding him that he was the richest person in the country. But the man couldn't sleep. He kept tossing and turning all night. Finally, he got out of bed and went to find the monk, who was sleeping under a tree. He woke the monk up, gave him back the diamond and said: "Give me the inner riches that make it possible for you to give this stone away."

Perhaps the monk has given us the secret of what we must discover if we want to find joy — real joy!

Balance is so hard to maintain in our own lives. We get busy. Demands are made of us. We have our own agendas, and we want to accomplish certain things. We drive ourselves, but sometimes we don't even know where we are going. Learning how to keep balance in our lives takes skill.

I learned what balance is from my friend Nancy, who was a Sister of St. Joseph. She was diagnosed with cancer of the hip on April 7, her 50th birthday. She lived only until July 16. One of the greatest gifts of my life is that during that short time, I managed to visit her three or four times a week. This was no easy task since she lived in a city more than two hours away. Somehow, I managed to find routes to take me in that direction. Even when I was headed in the other direction, I found creative ways to get back there.

When I would leave Nancy, my heart would be heavy. I would feel sad and devastated and angry. I wondered how something like this could happen to someone who was so good. She was always there to be of service and to walk with others through their pain. Now, she was experiencing pain that could never be truly defined. As I would drive back home, I would cry and talk out loud, trying to get the sadness out of me.

One of my trips to her house is a memory I will always cherish. As I walked into Nancy's room, she said, "Hi, Annie. I'm so glad you're here. Would you pick me up and carry me into the bathroom?" Of course, I would. After all, she was my friend!

After carrying her into the bathroom, cleaning her up and freshening up her bed, I said, "Nancy, we've got to talk about this anger." Nancy quickly responded, "Anger? What anger? I'm not angry!" Of course not. Nancy never got angry! I said, "Nancy, what do you mean you're not angry? You can't walk into the bathroom by yourself! You keep telling me that the Sisters bring you in food and say you must eat it."

That was the trigger. She said, "If they bring me in one more carrot and tell me it's good for cancer...." And then Nancy started talking about anger and all the things that she heroically had kept bottled up inside of her. After about two hours of this wonderful sharing, I said, "You know, Nancy, we have to keep laughing! What can we do to make sure we're laughing?"

Nancy had a reply: "Stop asking me these questions and go home." I quickly responded, "Okay." But Nancy added, just as quickly, "Stop asking, but don't go home." I knew I had pushed my friend long and hard enough.

A few days later, Nancy was taken to a hospital in a city that was even farther from me. After a few weeks, we began to make preparations to bring her back to the residence where our retired and ill Sisters reside. The day before bringing her home, I made one last trip. As I walked into her hospital room, there were twenty-two Sisters visiting her. (There's something you need to know about Sisters: When someone is in the hospital, everyone visits — whether it's sensible and appropriate or not!)

As I stood at the door of her room, Nancy smiled and said, "Annie, I'm so glad you're here." When I went over to my friend and kissed her, she whispered, "Get all these people out of here!" I whispered back, "I can't. But sit back and relax, and I'll entertain for a while.'"

When there were only a few people left in the room, Nancy taught me what balance is. She said, "You know, I was doing one of those Bernie Siegel exercises — the one where you walk down a long corridor, and there is a door at the end of the corridor and a person with a message at the other side of the door that you need to hear."

Now, if you knew my friend Nancy, you would have thought that she would have already figured out who would be at the other side of the door and what the message would be. But, if you've ever done one of those Bernie Siegel exercises, you know it just doesn't happen that way.

Nancy said, "I don't know what the message means. I went down the corridor, and when I got to the other side of the door, you know who was standing there? It was me. And I was seven years old, and all I was doing was laughing. I kept rolling in leaves, and I was laughing. All I did was laugh. What does it mean?" Then she reflected: "How did I learn to be so serious? How did I learn to be such an adult? Why couldn't I remember that laughing and playing were just as important as being responsible?"

I could only say, "I don't know, Nance. But do you want to spend the rest of the time we have laughing?" And we did! We had eight more days, and we spent them laughing.

None of us knows how many more days we have left. We should spend them laughing.

Chapter Seven

&.

PRESCRIPTION FOR JOY

I t's hard to study laughter and humor and joy. Mark Twain said, "Studying humor is like dissecting a frog. When you're done, you understand it, but it's dead."

I believe we already have joy and humor inside of us. When we are healthy people, we let it come out, and we share our joy with others. We may not have much control over situations and occurrences, but we do have control over how we respond to them. The power is within us. All we have to do is nurture it and believe in it.

Sometimes, we can hold on to stories and experiences to give us energy and to bring a gentle smile to our face. We can bury them inside of us; then all we have to do is learn how to recall them. Norman Cousins, author and editor, taught us the value of this when he learned how to deal with a spinal disorder. When he was told that he had a one in 500 chance of getting better, he realized that much of what he was experiencing was a result of the negative stress in his life. So he mapped out a plan for himself and rented films that helped him laugh. His prescription was to put laughter in his life. He realized that ten minutes of belly laughs could get him two hours of uninterrupted sleep. And his prescription worked: He was cured. Why can't we learn from his experience?

We need to start each morning with a positive thought. I ask people to develop a very simple exercise for themselves. It can be used throughout the day, and it can produce marvelous results and tremendous highs. Here it is:

As soon as you wake up, get out of bed and STAND. Then BREATHE. And then SMILE.

It's not hard to remember: STAND, BREATHE, SMILE. Right after you brush your teeth, look in the mirror and repeat this simple little prescription: STAND, BREATHE, SMILE.

Throughout the day as you start to feel some tension in your neck or in your back, STAND, BREATHE, SMILE. It's a simple way to take care of yourself. It doesn't cost any money. Best of all, it's a conscious choice for good health.

We also need to surround ourselves with positive people. Why stay in the company of negative, complaining, unhappy people? All they do is suck our energy. Before long, we begin to feel and sound just like them. Then the world has two negative, complaining, unhappy people.

There was an old woman who lived in a dingy old hut and all she ever did was complain. Nothing was ever right, and she was always feeling sorry for herself. Her fairy godmother took pity on her one day. Waving her magic wand, she changed the dingy hut into a beautiful mansion. When the old woman walked around the mansion, she complained about its size. It took all her time to clean it. How could she ever have time for anything else? The fairy godmother, hearing her complain, again took pity on the woman and swished her magic wand over the mansion. Immediately, it was filled with servants. Now the servants could attend to the large house, leaving the woman free. But she then began to gripe about how lazy all the servants were. All of her time was spent in organizing them, checking up on them, and making sure they finished their chores. One last time, the fairy godmother took out her magic wand. She waved it over the beautiful mansion filled with servants — and it became a small dingy hut....

That old woman chose unhappiness. She got more out of being unhappy. A lot of people are like that. It's a good idea to avoid them as much as we can. There is a wonderful principle for handling stress that states: "Don't waste your time trying to befriend a mad dog."

Sometimes, we want people or things to be different. We look for nurturing from another person or from an accomplishment, and we just don't find it. If the person chooses not to be there for us or if the job is unsatisfying, we might have to teach ourselves to walk away from it. Some things, some people, some dreams and some plans just don't work the way we want them to. In that case, we shouldn't try to befriend that person, job or dream. We should leave it.

Hold on to healthy messages instead. Hold on to stories and experiences and peak moments that give you joy and bring laughter to your soul. I was giving a lecture at an all-day conference for women that was sponsored by a hospital. One of the other presentations was given by a young doctor from Atlanta who presented his latest research on osteoporosis. The audience listened intently as he lectured from slides which listed the causes of osteoporosis for women.

I studied the list:

- "Petite." I was in no danger there!

- "Vegetarian diet." Saved again!

- "Exercise." Now I was beginning to like his research a lot!

I began to read ahead. Heading the second column on the slide was:

- "Obesity." Okay, so now he would get me.

As he started to address the second column, he said, "Now, obesity. Oddly enough, that prevents osteoporosis." I shouted out loud: "All right!"

Now, I live with the wonderful piece of information that I will never die of osteoporosis. Every time I hear the word, I smile. That's what I mean about holding on to things that bring you joy and relief. They not only free us; they also empower us, and allow us to be happier and more creative.

Chapter Eight

❧

BIFOCALS AND TRICK KNEES

W e live in a world of instant information. Every day, something new is printed to tell us how we can stay healthier. There are diet clubs and nutrition newsletters and talk shows galore on this topic. We are told that the slower the background music, the less people tend to eat at a meal. All one has to do is to watch an adolescent and listen to his background music to validate that statement.

We've held some myths for years and need to unlearn them in order to be healthier. For instance, spicy "hot" foods do not cause or aggravate ulcers; crackers and potato chips may be more likely to cause cavities than stickier foods like caramels and raisins. As we learn and relearn this information, we can make some other choices. Oddly enough, some of these choices are freeing. Others are delightful!

To experience joy in our lives, we must remember that we are connected to everything. We are in tune with the universe and the stars and the earth and the mountains and the oceans. We need to be one with ourselves, and to have a healthy respect and reverence for who we are. We have to be able to celebrate our gifts and talents while acknowledging our faults. We need to be in good relationships with other people. We are social beings who are not created to be alone. We need to be connected to other people. This is essential for us to be able to truly believe in who we are.

None of us can really own who we are unless we are validated by others. Someone can hope she is a good first grade teacher, but she can never really believe it unless someone validates that. This need for validation keeps us connected to each other. Relationships with others allow us to stretch ourselves and to learn to risk and to trust. It gets mighty risky sharing some deep, intimate feelings with another person because we become very vulnerable when we open ourselves up to someone else. However, if this never happens, there will be a part of us that is never alive. We must nurture and be nurtured. Joy can never come into our souls if we remain isolated and separate from others.

To have this joy, we must also have a belief in a power beyond ourselves. Wholeness calls us to be connected to our God. Joy is not connected to material possessions, nor is it measured by our accomplishments. Joy has nothing to do with what other people think of us. Joy is far beyond this:

- Joy is an inner state of being that gives life itself to our soul.

- Joy is woven into the very quality of our life.

- Joy is like the breath that keeps us connected to ourselves and to others.

• Joy makes our life meaningful and purposeful. If one chooses to see the meaning of life only in being useful and used, then one gets caught in a crisis of living. Therefore, joy and happiness and laughter and play give energy to our very bones!

Some people find it very threatening to realize that they need to be involved and connected to others. But Dr. Renee Spitz discovered that if human beings do not get significant recognition from others, their spines quite literally shrivel. They become increasingly withdrawn from relationships. That awareness puts a responsibility on all of our shoulders. It is important that we affirm and acknowledge other people who are in our lives.

Life is not a free ride. We all have to do our part. It is not only that I need to be recognized; I also have the responsibility to recognize those in my life. We are not in this alone. But what a wonderful thought! I need other people — and others need me!

Maybe it is not a coincidence that as we age, many of us need bifocals. Remembering your first pair of bifocals will bring images of the awkwardness of walking up and down stairs, shifting your head position to read newspapers and notices, and blurred vision that never existed before. But perhaps bifocals are just the reminders we need that we always have the ability to re-shape our vision. Bifocals are a reminder that we always have the ability to look at things differently and see different perspectives.

Aging, and even bifocals, can be real gifts. Aging is often intertwined with disease, but they are not the same. The average age at admission to nursing homes is not 65 or 70, but 80. Only five percent of the population is in some kind of institution, whether acute hospital, convalescent hospital, mental hospital, or nursing home. A recent Harris poll reported that only a little more than 20 percent of older Americans said they were debilitated by health problems. Recent research by the National Institute on Aging suggests that many of the problems of old age are not due to aging at all but to improper care of the body over a lifetime. Eighty percent of the health problems of older people are now thought to be preventable or postpone-able.

There is a story of an 82-year-old man who went to the doctor with the complaint that his left knee was painful and stiff. The man told the doctor that he just couldn't get comfortable. He couldn't stand or sit, and the knee was aching constantly. He asked the doctor to do something to relieve the pain. The doctor examined the man's knee and said, "Well, what do you expect? After all, it's an 82-year-old knee." The patient looked at the doctor and said, "Sure, it is, but so is the other one — and it's not bothering me!"

The more we talk about wellness and wholeness, the more we begin to understand the importance of keeping ourselves mentally alive and healthy. Most losses in mental capacity happen to the very old, not to people in their 60s, 70s and 80s, and those losses are due not to age itself but to depression, drug interactions, lack of exercise, or other reversible conditions.

Brain-scan studies conducted at the National Institute on Aging and based directly on metabolic activity have shown that "the healthy aged brain is as active and efficient as the healthy young brain." Study after study has shown that people who stay active and intellectually challenged not only maintain their mental alertness but also live longer.

Refocusing is a possibility for everyone. Even the most negative, unhappy, cynical person has the ability to refocus. Human beings have such power. We can blink our eyes. We can hold in our memories happy, joyful, lifegiving remembrances. Dr. Deepak Chopra in his best-selling book, "Ageless Body/Timeless Mind," tells the story of a woman who had open-heart surgery. At first, the body rejected the new heart. Then the body accepted it. When the woman woke up, she immediately asked for McDonald's hamburgers and beer. This woman had never liked either. But the man whose heart she had received had just left McDonald's when the fatal accident that cost him his life occurred. And he had loved beer!

Our organs hold on to our memories. We walk with our past inside our very being. We have to respect and reverence those memories, to hold on to those which are life-giving, and to release the negative ones from our bodies. If only we would heed the words of anthropologist Ashley Montagu when he suggested that we should all try to "die young as late as possible." And we could all learn a lesson from comedian George Burns, who said: "You can't help getting older, but you can help getting old."

Joy and humor can be a wonderful way of adding years to your life. More importantly, they may add life to your years.

Chapter Nine

— ❧ —

BE 'ANGRY SMART'

Anger can block our senses. We hear only the words that have hurt us. We hold on to memories that speak to us of disappointing events. We remember when we were passed over for a job or when a relationship ended. We recall our disappointments and failures. Recalling such things, people stop speaking to each other. Or they belittle others and tell family members or friends or anyone who will listen unkind things about another who is responsible for the anger.

What begins to happen is that people let anger become a part of them. But the only one who suffers from the anger is the person who holds onto it.

There are virtually no benefits in holding onto anger. It eats away only at the person who chooses to hold onto it. Some people tell every available ear the story over and over and over again. The only thing that does is rehearse the anger. There is no therapeutic value in it. It does not release the anger. It only builds a larger pot of anger and creates more of a case for one to be angry.

There isn't a person alive that has not felt anger.

Anger, in itself, is not bad. No feeling has a moral judgment attached to it. It is not the feeling we are responsible for, but the behavior we choose to deal with the feeling. You can't help it if you're cold or hot. You just are. But if you choose to walk naked down a street because you are hot, you will be judged.

Anger is really a secondary feeling. It's a display of your real feeling. The next time you feel anger, stop yourself and ask what else you feel. Maybe you feel angry because you're disappointed things didn't work out as you would have liked them to. Or maybe you are angry because you are frustrated. You have asked to have something done over and over, and it never gets done. Or maybe you feel angry because you feel so helpless and powerless. If you can begin to look at what else is under your anger, you will begin to understand the feeling.

Some people use anger to intimidate or scare another. Anger can be manipulative and destructive. Anger can grow into rage or violence. It's not uncommon to see broken bones, holes in walls, gunshot wounds or smashed cars as the results of anger that has gone out of control. Some use anger to bully or threaten others. Situations get out of control, and people display a great insensitivity towards the victim of their anger.

Anger sometimes results in people no longer communicating with each other. There are many ways this happens:

• Some people stop communicating by no longer using words to convey their messages. They stop speaking.

- Others use blame as their mode of attack.

- Sarcasm is another style of not communicating properly; mean, hurtful statements are sent in to attack the other person.

- Instead of complaining and fighting, other people deal with their anger by "being nice." They attempt to avoid anger at all costs. These people often act hurt or tearful. This "being quiet" and "not saying anything" is frequently done so one will not "rock the boat." It's the "peace at any price" theory. But the "nicer" these people become, the more they grow in rage, resentment and unconscious anger. If, per chance, anger comes out, then they are ridden with guilt. Guilt is a way for them not to get in touch with their own anger because it is impossible to be angry and guilty.

All of these methods of non-communication are paralyzing for the other person, who is left helpless and without any information. Hence, it becomes impossible to come to a resolution. The healthy choice is to be in touch with what makes us angry and to look at behaviors we choose to deal with it. Some of us choose unhealthy ways to cope.

One way to view anger is to see our behaviors in one of two categories: "angry smart" or "angry dumb."

- When we choose "angry smart" behaviors, we resolve the situation. We deal with the person we need to. We can move out of anger and not get stuck in the feeling. There is no need to be bitter or resentful or depressed. Some people internalize the anger, and it becomes a depression. There is a heavy price to pay for that choice. Take your pick: ulcers, migraine headaches, heart attacks, colitis — to mention just a few. But "angry smart" means there is a resolution. Nothing gets buried inside of us. The anger is not left boiling and bubbling and then exploding.

• "Angry dumb" means we make choices that are unhealthy for ourselves and for others. We break something or throw something or destroy something. This type of anger is destructive to all parties involved. It can involve physical acting out. But the worst part of "angry dumb" behaviors is that they eat away at people.

The destruction of "angry dumb" is not only of a physical nature. Psychologically, the price if very heavy. Voice levels are out of control. Choices of words include zingers that are hurtful and cutting. Tenderness, sensitivity, intimacy, warmth, caring and love are absent.

Joy, laughter and humor are hard to find when you are angry. Anger is like a brick wall, and it gets very hard to see over it, around it or beyond it. Staying in the anger, one chooses to remain unhappy and unhealthy. To free ourselves of this and to opt for life and life-giving moments, it's important to deal with anger and what creates it for us.

Here are a few suggestions for freeing yourself of anger and opting for joy. Think of your situations and apply these ideas to yourself. Some may fit; others may not. Some may fit today while some may be options for tomorrow:

• TAKE A TIME OUT. Very often, we are so angry when we act that we behave irrationally. Taking a few minutes of "cooling off" time is helpful and beneficial. Go for a twenty-minute walk. People say things they really don't mean when they're angry. Then reset a time to bring the situation to some conclusion.

• YOU HAVE THE RIGHT TO SPEAK OUT and voice your opinion. We really fail ourselves when we do not stand up for what we believe.

• DO NOT SWALLOW YOUR ANGER. Identify what your anger is all about. Clarify your own issues. State, as directly as possible, what you are talking about so the other person can understand it.

• TALK OUT YOUR ANGER. Name what it is you are angry about. Rehearse it, if necessary, in front of a mirror. Be clear in sending the message.

• DON'T USE RIDICULE or labeling when talking about your anger. The hearer will not be able to understand your message because he will get caught in the label or the put-down. That only raises the defensiveness. Nothing will get solved.

• BLAMING, PREACHING, moralizing, lecturing, interpreting, and diagnosing will be perceived only as put-downs. It is important not to use statements that make the hearer feel that she is being attacked. People don't keep their ears open when they think they are being judged.

• SPEAK FOR YOURSELF. We never have the right to speak for someone else. The use of "I" messages can help you stay on target. When a sentence begins with "I," the listener doesn't feel that a finger-pointing blame message is being sent.

• ALLOW THE OTHER PERSON to have his own feelings. Don't discount those feelings. Don't criticize the feelings, and don't tell people they have no right to their feelings.

• WRITE OUT YOUR ANGER. Write a letter to the person you are angry at. Tell her everything you want her to know. Just let yourself write. Spelling doesn't count. You are also free to use any language that you want. Just keep writing until you feel that you've written enough. Then read the letter. You will be surprised at what you've written. Your handwriting will even look different to you. After you have read the letter, tear it up in as many little pieces as possible and throw it away. It is very important that this step be followed. Do not save it until the next day to read again. Do not send the letter to the person to whom you have written it. The purpose of this exercise is to get the anger out of you. It will also clarify some issues for you.

• FIND ONE OTHER PERSON you can tell the story to. Speak as honestly as possible to this person. Tell him every piece of your story. However, it is very important that you choose to do this exercise with only one person. If you tell another, then another and then another, all you have done is rehearse your anger. That is non-productive.

• IDENTIFY THE PAY-OFFS in not dealing with your anger. Some people choose to hang onto the anger. They get something out of it. Figure out what it is.

• GO OUT and do some physical activity. Go for a walk or jog or shoot some baskets. Find a pond and throw some stones. Cut the grass. Shovel some snow. Go swimming. Play golf.

• LISTEN. If the anger is from the other person towards you, then you need to listen to what she is saying. Don't interrupt her. Try to hear the message as objectively as possible. Allow her to have her own opinion.

• WATCH YOUR TONE of voice. Yelling only produces yelling. Screaming blocks ears. Repeating what you need to say as briefly as possible in a tone of voice that is as soft as you can manage makes it more likely that the other person will listen and really hear what has been said.

Chapter Ten

❧

ACCENT ON STRESS

S tress is a killer. It affects the quality of many lives. It would be impossible to find anyone in the world who does not experience some level of stress and anxiety. But stress can be dealt with. And if we don't deal with it, it begins to deal with us.

There is a positive stress called "eustress." It helps us to function and to get things accomplished. It's the stress we all feel when we walk into a dinner party or a meeting and begin to wonder if we will know anyone or if we will feel out of place. It is the stress we feel when we've just started a better job. It's the stress experienced at the birth of a baby. It's the stress a student feels when writing a term paper. We've all had similar experiences and know the effects of this type of stress on us.

Stress is your body's physical, mental and chemical reaction to circumstances that excite, confuse, frighten, endanger or irritate you. Stress can be caused by an identified or unidentified stressor or by a stressful event. It is impossible to go through life without stress since stress prepares us to handle things that are unfamiliar and things that appear to threaten us.

Faced with a crisis — emotional or physical — the human body has a fairly standard physical reaction: arousal hormones pour into the blood stream...the heart beats faster...blood pressure rises...the lungs suck in more oxygen...more sugar circulates in the blood to provide energy. This is the "Fight or Flight" response that gets the body ready for action and, in some circumstances, could save your life. But if the strain continues, it is very possible that a serious illness may result.

Not everyone reacts to stress the same way. Some people thrive on stress while others fall apart under it. Researchers have discovered that it's mostly a matter of how you handle it. There is ample evidence to prove that stress can contribute to various medical problems: heart disease, high blood pressure, ulcers, asthma, headaches, and even the common cold.

"Eustress" is the stress of winning. It comes with a sense of achievement, triumph and exhilaration. "Distress" is the negative stress. This is the stress of losing. It occurs when one senses a loss of feelings of security and adequacy. Disappointments, feelings of desperation and a sense of helplessness can trigger distress.

People today are feeling a great deal of stress in relation to the workplace. They take on too much for too long and too intensely. Then they begin to feel a lot of pressure. This pressure comes from three places: within, without, and administration.

One feels pressure from within to accomplish and

to succeed. The pressure one experiences from without is from the population the person is trying to serve. Administration pressures others by demanding and judging on statistics and playing the numbers game. When that happens, the person begins to feel more guilt. As a result, one puts in more and more hours, puts forth more effort, and tries harder and harder. Thus the person begins to work harder, and becomes more exhausted, frustrated, irritable and cynical in his outlook and behavior. This results in a less effective person.

Hans Selye, who has been called the "Father of Stress" (I wonder if it stressed him to have that nickname), attempted with the General Adaptation Syndrome to explain stress to us. There are three stages: the alarm stage, the stage of resistance, and the stage of exhaustion:

• The alarm stage occurs when one first notices a stressor and prepares to fight it. This is the short period when the adrenalin starts to flow.

• One then moves into the stage of resistance. Our bodies give us extra strength to get through the crisis period.

• The final stage is exhaustion when the crisis is over and we just can't go on anymore. If we don't plan time for the exhaustion stage, our bodies take over by getting sick and forcing us to take a rest.

Stress is going to happen to us, but it doesn't have to kill us. The following are a few suggestions for handling and dealing with stress. Some may fit your circumstances while others may not:

• KNOW WHAT CAUSES your stress. Identify the situations in your life that make you feel tense. This is a very important step but one we tend to skip over. We think we know the stress and never look at the cause of it. It's not the stress you know about that's going to get you; it's the stress you don't know about.

• IDENTIFY YOUR FEELINGS. Feelings are important to understand because they determine your behaviors. Once you are aware of your feelings, you get an insight into your choices of behaviors.

• BECOME AWARE of your body and such signs as headaches, tensed muscles, stomach upsets, cold or clammy hands, and clenched teeth. Those are signals from the body that indicate the presence of stress in your life.

• WE ALL RESPOND to stressful situations either physically, mentally, or both physically and mentally. We need to react to the stress in the very same way. If your body wiggles and you can't sit still, then you respond to stress in a physical manner. If your mind goes thirty miles an hour and you can't concentrate, then you respond mentally to stressful situations.

Research has helped us look at the necessity of choosing behaviors that match our reaction. If you respond physically, then get up and walk slowly for about a minute or two. The anxiety will then begin to decrease. Then you can ask yourself what the stress is all about.

If your mind keeps going and you can't sleep, then open a book. This should be a book for entertainment and not something you are studying or want to remember the contents of. A good novel does the trick. Read and read and read, and then you will begin to feel the anxiety subside. At that point, you can then ask yourself what is causing the stress.

If you respond both physically and mentally to stress, then put activities in your life that require both physical and mental reactions. Swimming, dancing and playing tennis are examples of activities that require both physical and mental behaviors.

• MEMORIZE THIS: "Things worth doing are worth doing poorly." Obviously, this is not what we were taught. We believe that we have to have all the time necessary to complete a project or else we don't even start it. Hence, many things never get accomplished. We need to learn to use our time well. If we have only twenty minutes, then using that time guarantees that twenty minutes of the project gets done. People look out at their gardens and think, "I have to weed the whole garden." Why not pull out just the big weeds? When we are having company, we say, "I have to polish all the silverware." Why not polish only what you are going to use?

• ASK YOURSELF: "What's the worst possible thing that can happen?" It usually is not a catastrophe. The result may not exactly be what I want or expected, but it is not worth all the negative energy to worry about it.

• MAKE A LIST of things that uplift you...things that bring a smile to your face...things that make you feel good and appreciated and cared about: a sunrise, a sunset, a compliment, getting an unexpected phone call from a friend, receiving a card in the mail or a letter from someone who is thinking about you, watching a humorous movie, having someone remember your birthday. Make up your own list. Then watch how some of those things happen without your getting the mileage you could out of them. Use them. They really are stress reducers.

• LISTEN to your own "self-talk." That's the talk or conversation that goes on in your head all the time. If that self-talk is negative, then your stress level will remain very high. If you hear yourself being negative, change it to positive self-talk.

• CHECK OUT YOUR EXPECTATIONS. We have expectations for everything. We expect to drive home safely from work, we expect people we love to love us back, we expect people to be on time for appointments, we expect people to be honest with us — the list could go on forever. The next time you get upset or frustrated, check out the expectations that you had. When our expectations are not met, some type of crisis comes into our life. This crisis usually takes the form of sadness, frustration or anger.

• MAKE A DISTINCTION for yourself between wants and needs. We do not "need" everything. We may "want" something, but we really don't "need" it. Needs keep us in the compulsion area. There is no choice in this area. If you need something, you cannot live without it. We all need air, food, water and to be touched physically. We do not need to drive Lincolns, to own fur coats, or to eat gourmet meals each evening. We may want those things, but we truly do not need them.

• DEVELOP A BELIEF in your own competence.

Everyone has some competence in some area. Some people can bake pies, others write books; some fly planes, others have computer skills; many excel in sports. Find at least one thing you can do and celebrate that.

• CHANGE IRRATIONAL THOUGHTS and ideas into rational ones. Some people cling to thoughts that bind them: "I have to be perfect"..."People should act the way I want them to"..."I have to have everyone's love and approval." Messages like those lead to unhealthy and fragmented lives. Change such irrational messages to: "It's human to make mistakes and I'm not bad because I am not perfect"..."People act the way they want to act and not the way I want them to act"..."It would be nice to have others' approval and love, but even without it I can still be okay." The last three offer a healthier and happier life.

• KNOW YOUR OWN SUPPORT SYSTEMS and creatively use them. Find the people who are supportive of you and find ways to connect with them. This connection does not have to be time-consuming. A few minutes of conversation that touches your heart is worth a fortune. Telephones, letters, lunches, meetings, parties and vacations are a few ways of making these connections. Be as creative as possible in making your own list.

• STAY INVOLVED and active. Feeling productive reduces stress. Don't just sit and listen to music; instead, learn to play a musical instrument. If you are not athletically inclined, buy a season pass to a sporting event and cheer for your team.

• ORGANIZE your time well. Make a list of all the

things you need to accomplish each morning. Then code them. Things that absolutely and positively have to get done that day are number one. The two's on your list can be important things but not essential. The three's are things that will probably get on tomorrow's list. You accomplish more items on your list if you take the time to prioritize them. That also helps your self-esteem because you feel good about all you got accomplished versus putting yourself down by reading your list at the end of the day and making note of all the things that never got done.

• BE CLEAR. If the stress you are experiencing is a result of poor communication, then it is necessary to send clear, direct, honest messages to clear up the problem. Asserting oneself is a skill. It requires that you be in touch with your own choice of words and listen to your own tone of voice in sending the message.

But be clear about this: Assertiveness is not aggressiveness. If you are aggressive, you really don't care about the other person. If you are submissive or passive, you really don't care about yourself; you think everyone else is more important. But when you choose to be assertive, you respect yourself and the other person. Then both can win.

• DEVELOP DAILY HABITS that contribute to health. Good nutrition and healthy eating are essential to wholeness and happiness. You should have some regular exercise in your daily routine. Good habits should include some play time. We need time to relax our muscles and clear the cobwebs out of our brains. Laughter does this well! We also need some relaxation in our daily routine. For some, this may be time spent reading the paper or a book; for others, it may be sitting in a recliner doing nothing.

• GET TO LIKE YOURSELF. There are good things about you, and you should be proud on them. Affirm yourself. Pat yourself on the back.

• GET ENTHUSIASTIC. When we begin anything, we will always find a high level of enthusiasm. Think of a significant person in your life. Do you remember when you met that person? Wasn't he or she just wonderful? You found excuses to call that person several times a day, and sent cards and gifts for no reason. Try doing some of those things you used to do for that special person in your life and watch the relationship be energized. Think of when you began the job you are in right now. Do you remember how you went home and told everyone how nice the place was and how special the people were who worked there? Enthusiasm can be regained.

• START IDENTIFYING and appreciating differences in people. We sometimes get our stress levels high because we think differences are wrong or negative. Differences can enhance our relationships. A respect of differences can make our work places easier for all of us. Differences are not bad. The acknowledgment and acceptance of individual differences will decrease our stress and anxiety level. Remember that acceptance does not imply that you agree with everything. It is possible to accept someone and not agree with him.

Chapter Eleven

❧

AMANDA'S SNOW CONES

W e all experience losses and must endure suffering through them. This process begins at birth and is, as a matter of fact, the first experience we have when we lose the security and protection of our mother's womb. As our life unfolds, we continue to face losses. These losses have many faces: the death of significant people...friends moving away...the betrayal of false friends...physical losses, such as sickness, loss of eyesight, loss of hearing, aging...and our personal losses.

The challenge for all of us is to cope and deal with the loss, and to begin to allow the hurt to heal. This does not happen overnight. As a matter of fact, there is no single timeline which predicts this process. Each one of us is different; we each walk — and heal — to our own drummer.

To begin dealing with the loss, we much first acknowledge it. It is important that we "own" the loss. Many try to deny it or hope the pain of it will go away. However, reality doesn't disappear, even when it's painful. We must talk about our losses and admit they are real. Loss hurts! The pain can be intolerable.

Denial doesn't make it disappear. Neither does ignoring it and saying, "Just don't think about it. There's nothing you can do about it." That attitude just prolongs the pain. Some people try to endure the pain alone and so internalize it. Those are the people who pay a price by getting physically sick and depressed. For us to be healthy and happy, we must make a choice to deal with the loss.

Acknowledging a loss implies being in touch not only with the loss itself but also with our feelings. It is all right to feel angry; to experience sadness, hurt and resentment; to be disappointed and frustrated. We have a right to our feelings. Feelings are never right or wrong. They just are. No moral judgment can be placed on feelings. Feelings just come, and it is for us to be in touch with what they are. You can't help your feelings. As a matter of fact, you cannot even become aware of your feelings until you experience them. The problem then is to identify the feeling.

It is not unusual for people to experience numbness or a sense of shock when a loss occurs. That deadens the pain. If you've ever gone through the loss of someone you love dearly, the numbness gets you through the initial stages. The feeling of grief usually follows this numbness. It is very important for us to release the pain through tears and not keep it bottled up inside of us in an attempt to be strong.

Next, it is common for people to experience a sense of being alone or forsaken. Often, that feels like depression. At this stage, one experiences a helplessness or heaviness and does not feel her "normal self." It is important not to anesthetize these feelings with unhealthy behaviors like eating too much or not at all, drinking to excess, smoking, sleeping too much or not at all. Those only prolong our grieving process. These unhealthy Band-Aids do not deal with loss in a positive way. It is not uncommon at this stage to develop unhealthy relationships. People grab on to another person hoping this will ease the pain of the loss. This is an attempt to fill a void that one experiences because of the loss.

Physical symptoms can begin to surface. Headaches, loss of appetite, insomnia and stomachaches are common physical expressions of unresolved grief. What scares people at this stage is that it is almost impossible to concentrate on anything. They begin to think they are "going crazy."

In an attempt to deal with the pain of loss, some people choose to hold on to guilt. Guilt is a way of not having to deal with anger. It's impossible to feel guilt and anger at the same time. Sometimes, the guilt is from what one said or did not say; this is an attempt to blame oneself. Guilt can be irrational, exaggerated and neurotic. One can certainly get stuck in guilt.

We can also choose to blame the other person for the loss. Then we will experience feelings of hostility and resentment. It ends up being the "fault" of someone else. Now we have the right to look sad, throw temper tantrums, sulk and look unhappy. Sometimes, this is an attempt to make others feel some guilt or at least feel bad. It can be controlling and manipulative.

To deal with loss, we must learn to start again. Starting again offers us the ability to see options, to care and to feel alive again. Dealing with a loss means letting go of our pain so the pain does not own us. Dealing with a loss means learning to forgive. All of this takes time.

Our losses include not only our separations and departures from those we lose but also our conscious and unconscious losses as well: of our dreams, our impossible expectations, our illusions of freedom and power, and our younger selves.

We are constantly growing because we leave and let go and lose. We must mourn the loss of others and the loss of ourselves. The changes in our body re-define us. The events of our personal history re-define us. We are always dealing with letting go: of our waistlines, our vigor, our sense of adventure, our 20/20 vision, our playfulness, our trust, our dreams.

The following are some practical ways of dealing with loss. Do not limit yourself to these suggestions. Listen to yourself and others, and find what helps you through this process:

- Identify the loss. Name it.

- Look for options that are available to you.

- Re-invest in your work.

- Get re-involved in activities that are life-giving and happy for you.

- Re-connect with friends.

- Volunteer your time. Give some of you away. You'll feel connected to others. Volunteering also broadens your viewpoints and experiences. It helps give you a new perspective on things.

- Realize that all people have limits. Look at your own realistically.

- If you have a hobby or some special interest, spend some time developing it. If you need to, learn a new one.

- Express your feelings out loud. Find someone you can trust and who can truly listen to you (and not just try to make you feel better or talk you out of your feelings). It's even helpful for you to talk about your feelings out loud to yourself. Talk to a mirror or just listen to what you are saying to yourself. This can help clarify what you are really experiencing.

- Be kind to yourself. Do things you like to do. Treat yourself to your favorite meal.

- Get plenty of rest. Physically and psychologically, you get drained when dealing with loss; you need to give yourself some extra rest time.

- Take a course or learn some skill you have always wanted to take the time to learn.

- Take all the hugs you can get. Hugs are worth a million words.

- Set a few new goals. Beginnings have energy, and new experiences give us life.

- Look at photographs and listen to music that was important to you. It helps you look at the problem head on.

- Remember that grieving and dealing with loss takes time. It is a process. Be patient with yourself.

Eventually, the process does end. It does not go on forever — unless you let that happen. Sometimes, you get more by holding on to pain, so you never let go. Maybe this gets you more attention or offers you an excuse to stay removed and non-productive. But loss and grieving do end. Then something new comes to us.

Perhaps that's the message of the silkworm. The silkworm come from a seed about the size of a grain of pepper. When the warm weather comes and the leaves begin to appear on the mulberry tree, the seeds start to live. Until then, they were dead. The worms nourish themselves on mulberry leaves until, having grown to full size, they settle on some twigs. Then, using their mouths, they go about spinning the silk and making some very thick little cocoons in which they enclose themselves. The fat, ugly silkworm then dies, and a beautiful little white butterfly comes forth from the cocoon.

Trying to understand loss and its pieces allows the pain to change. I learned this a few years ago. My father was hit by a car in January 1983. The girl who hit him was on her way bowling and never saw him crossing the street. My father never left the ICU of the hospital and died that April. Throughout those three months, we never heard from or met the girl who was driving the car.

Nine years later, I was giving a lecture and was seated at a large round table for dinner. All the participants had on name tags, and I began reading the names of the people at the table with me. Directly across from me was a woman who had the same

71

name as the person who hit my father. Was she the same person? I dismissed the thought. After I finished the dinner talk, several people stood in line to talk with me. Toward the end of the line was the woman.

She said, "Was your father hit by a car on January 10, 1983?" As I said "yes," she burst into tears and said, "I am the one who hit your father." I quickly put my arm around her and told her how grateful I was that she came up to me and then started to fill in the pieces that he had died. She already knew.

She said, "I was on my way bowling and wasn't paying any attention. All of a sudden, your father was in my windshield. I jumped out and started to yell for help, but there was no one around. I asked him not to die and took off my jacket and put it over him and kept asking him to wait for help."

I then decided we needed to get out of the room we were in, and so I started to walk out with her. I asked her to forgive herself. I tried to assure her that no one was holding it against her and that my father had died very peacefully. As we walked through the doorway, someone pulled me back for a second and the woman continued to leave the building. I don't remember her name anymore. It's not important anymore. I will always be grateful that she told me she put her jacket on him and kept talking to him.

When you are dealing with loss, be sure to ask for help. This is not an easy thing for most adults. It is much easier to help someone else. But asking for help keeps you in touch with where you are. It also allows others to be there for you. Asking for help really empowers the requester.

I learned that lesson from eight-year-old Amanda, who was very frightened while in the hospital. About a week after she went blind, the doctors decided to put in a central line to facilitate administering medication and food to her. Her Mom left us alone in the hospital room so we could visit a while. As soon as Amanda found out we were alone, she began talking about some things that were bothering her. She finally got to talking about her fears about the central line. I admitted I, too, would be afraid if I were having the procedure done and encouraged her to continue talking about it. She then taught me a wonderful lesson. She said, "Anne, teach me something so I don't have to be afraid."

I said, "Okay. Tell me someone that when that person is with you, you feel safe and secure. You feel protected."

Quickly, she responded, "My Mom."

I continued, "Now give me something — a thing — that when you have it, you feel good and happy. It brings a smile to your face and you feel the giggles inside, too."

Just as quickly as before, she responded, "Snow cones."

I said, "Now do this with me. Tomorrow, they are going to come in and get you and put you on a stretcher and start to push you down the corridor. You'll feel scared and frightened — and that's okay. Now they're pushing you — and oh, look, Amanda, look who's coming down the hall towards you! It's your Mom. And look, Amanda, what's that she has in her hand? It's a snow cone!"

Amanda smiled a smile that lit up the whole room and won my heart. She yelled, "Yeah, Anne, it's a rainbow snow cone."

Assuring her, I said, "Yes, it's a rainbow snow cone."

Amanda then said, "Stop, Anne. It works. It's okay."

A few minutes later, when her mother returned, Amanda said, "Mom, I want to tell you something so you don't have to be scared."

For Amanda, it worked. And all she had to do was ask!

Chapter Twelve

❧

HEALTHY 'I' AND HEALTHY 'WE'

R elationships are funny things. You can't live with them and you can't live without them. They are capable of bringing both joy and sadness into our lives. They can also bring us energy or drain us. We cry because of things that occur in our relationships, and we laugh together in the same relationships.

We do not have many positive models for relationships in our culture. What we see are unhealthy relationships. We see abuse and violence and dysfunctional patterns. We witness people casting away relationships. Divorce occurs on many levels:

• People stop talking to each other.

• People go years without even remembering what caused the division for them.

• Some find themselves lonely because they shy away from intimacy and closeness.

• Others are afraid of commitment and go from one relationship to another, inventing reasons not to bond.

Enduring the growth of a relationship has been lost

in a culture that thinks things should happen quickly and easily, or maybe it's not worth it. Look around your kitchen at the appliances: electric can openers, dishwashers, microwave ovens. They all imply a "hurry-up attitude." We no longer sit on our front porches in rocking chairs and enjoy conversations with family members and friends. Instead, we blast our televisions and radios, and walk around with headphones stapled to our ears.

What are we afraid of? Is it life itself? Is it each other? Is it ourselves?

Relationships take a long time to mature. Adolescents often think if they go out twice with someone, they are "going steady." The art of building friendships and relationships is lost. Often, people jump into a sexual relationship and don't take the time to build the relationship on other levels. "Dear Abby" had a "gem of the day" quote in the newspaper that could challenge all of us: "It takes a long time to grow an old friend."

When we begin a relationship, we get into an enmeshment stage. During this time, we lose the concept of self and tend to identify ourselves in relation to the other. During this stage, we have a lot of intimacy but no autonomy. We experience a lot of closeness. However, we do not set any personal boundaries. This is a very romantic model. It appears to be like love. It is at this stage that we see very dependent relationships. It is also during this stage that you can't choose to love the other since you need the other. Negative feelings are not expressed at this stage.

While in the enmeshment stage, thoughts of the other person are very frequent. People call the other a thousand times a day. They bring home flowers and gifts. Cards are picked out especially for the other. The problem is that it is impossible for both people to remain in this stage. Inevitably, one will outgrow it.

When that occurs, we have a tendency to jump to disengagement. Now there is no closeness. There is a lot of autonomy but no intimacy. This stage is defined as the "I do my thing; you do your thing" stage. It is here we find divorce. And divorce happens in all kinds of relationships — marriages, families, friendships, work.

We have to find the balance of mutuality. This stage requires both autonomy and intimacy. I can have my own identity and think my own thoughts and make my own decisions. You can think your own thoughts and make your own decisions and have your own identity. You can't have a healthy "we" unless you have a healthy "I." But neither can you have a healthy "I" unless you have a healthy "we."

The following are a few suggestions to help create healthy relationships. Remember that relationships take a lot of work; none of these is meant to be used individually. It takes two people giving about 80 percent to each other to maintain any relationship. This list is for all kinds of relationships — marriage, significant others, friends, family members, God, community members:

• DEVELOP INTELLECTUAL INTIMACY with each other. Intellectual intimacy is how we talk to each other. It is sharing thoughts, ideas and opinions with someone we want to be close to. We can talk about politics, religion and the headlines in the news. We can discuss conditions of society, schools and families today. The topic is not important. It is the talking and sharing that begin to bond us. We begin to relate to each other. We sometimes forget to keep this process going when we begin getting used to each other.

In the early days of getting to know each other, we talk about almost anything just to be able to spend time with the other. As we get more comfortable with the other and get to know patterns of behavior, we talk less and less. Intellectual intimacy challenges us to stay in touch with the other. This is information that we learn from others or from the television or newspaper so it is not very threatening. Everyone is entitled to his or her own opinion.

• WE CAN GET CLOSER to each other as we share feelings with each other. Feelings are a different level of communication and far more risky to share than intellectual thoughts. We have a tendency not to share our feelings because we are much more vulnerable with the person to whom we reveal our feelings. However, to be close and have a healthy relationship with another, it is essential that we share this part of us with the other. There is no way we can truly know ourselves or another person unless we share our feelings.

• SHARING THE VALUES of the other is another way we can be bonded in a relationship. It means knowing the other and appreciating her or his interests. Those values do not need to become ours. They are the interests, loves and lifelines of the other. But we must learn to appreciate them. If our significant person enjoys music, then it is important that we (once in a while) go to a concert or listen to an important piece of music. If we like movies, then it is a reasonable request that the other (once in a while) go to a movie with us. Doing so even gives both something to discuss on an intellectual sharing level.

Values are at the core of who we are, so it is essential to share our values with people we love and for those same people to share their values with us. It is important that there be some common values also. These are the things both can then experience and enjoy together. You can begin to identify your values by looking how you spend your time and money. What are the ways you use your free time?

The "why" of anything tells about values. For instance, ask yourself what is your favorite television show and "why"; what is your favorite food and "why"; what is your favorite vacation place and "why". It is not your answer that helps you get to know yourself; it is the "why" behind it. To be able to be oneself and not have to disown one's values to please another is what intimate love is all about.

• LOOK AT YOUR OWN TRUST LEVELS in relationships. I cannot get close to another nor laugh and share life unless I trust the other. Sometimes, our capacity for trust is stilted by our own early upbringing. How we grew up, how we felt loved and how we experienced security are all essential for us to know ourselves and then share with one with whom we choose to be close and intimate. Family secrets can block us in our ability to give ourselves to others. This is not to imply we should be "open books" for everyone, but it is meant to be a red flag in relationships if we never reveal who we are to another.

The capacity for trust is also influenced by our own experiences with love. If you have been hurt or scared in a love relationship, you may not be too willing to enter another one for fear that this may happen again. It is helpful to reflect on our own history of relationships and to be aware of positive and negative aspects of these past relationships.

- LEARN THAT DIFFERENCES are not bad and can truly enhance a relationship. Learn all you can about the interests of the other and leave room for different likes and activities.

- LET THE OTHER PERSON MAKE MISTAKES. Don't be so fast in putting him down. We need to affirm each other and not disregard or judge each other.

- DON'T BRING PAST RESENTMENTS or arguments into the present. No one can change what happened yesterday. To keep nagging or bringing up what another did or didn't do changes nothing.

- FORGIVE THE OTHER. Forgiveness is a conscious act. It is not a feeling. Decide that you care enough about the other that you can forgive and let go. Remember that forgiveness and the ability to forget are not the same. We don't always forget the behavior, but we can still forgive.

- HUG AND TOUCH. From birth, we have physical needs. We all need to be touched and hugged. In a relationship, it is essential to put your arm around the other person once in a while. Physical expressions of love speak volumes of words. This physical intimacy is different from sexual intimacy. No one can survive without physical intimacy.

• THE WORDS "I'M SORRY" are not a sign of weakness. They are a sign of courage and strength. To admit you are wrong takes courage. However, one can mistakenly believe that saying, "I'm sorry" is all that's needed. To say it once is fine. After that, a behavior must accompany the words. For example, if a waiter spills hot tea on my arm and says, "I'm sorry," I hope he is, but it is not enough. My arm must be attended to.

• CLARIFY EXPECTATIONS. What do I expect from you? What do you expect from me? Are these real or unreal? Can I be open to change any expectations that are unreal? If not, I will remain frustrated.

• RELATIONSHIPS NEED TO HAVE SELF-REVELATION from both people. That takes time. Time must be spent nourishing and nurturing the relationship. Time is needed to celebrate the relationship. It is in using this time together and focusing on the other that one grows in the relationship.

• GO SLOWLY. Relationships mature slowly and must be nurtured gently.

Chapter Thirteen

NOW HEAR THIS

Every second of our lives, we communicate. Sometimes, we are aware of how we are communicating and how we are coming across to the other. At other times, we aren't. There are times we are aware of another's communication to us. At other times, we just block out the messages.

All of us have experienced the effects of poor communications. People feel not heard...feelings get hurt...no one understands...no one cares...harsh and mean words are spoken. Sometimes, silence, that dreadful absence of any communication, ices over people.

There are many maxims about communication:

1. When communication is on target, people resolve differences and share openly, directly and honestly with each other.

2. Some communications are serious and come complete with agendas. Other communications are just plain fun and filled with laughter and nonsense.

3. Some communications are hurtful and destructive.

4. Relationships are defined by the quality of com-

munication between the people involved. Work situations, and even the quality of the work, are determined by the communication that exists.

5. The way we communicate is an indicator of our own self-esteem and self-confidence.

There is never a moment of our lives that we are not communicating. We were born to be communicators. We communicate using words, and we communicate nonverbally — all at the same time. Each communication is composed of both verbal and nonverbal messages. Seven percent of our communication is verbal. That means that 93 percent is nonverbal. Fifty-eight percent of the message comes to us through body posture, facial expressions, gestures, eye contact and distance. Thirty-five percent of our communication is in tonality.

If one were to use a pie concept, it would look like the following:

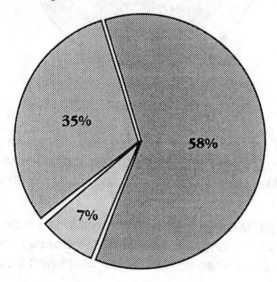

The distance we are from someone else is also significant. People use space as a buffer between themselves and other people. Some people manipulate the space to send messages. The following diagram indicates various distances and the relationship that results:

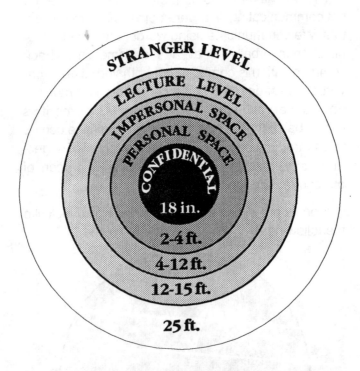

As we allow people to come closer to us, we are allowing them into our lives. This is a process which involves several stages which can actually be measured:

• STRANGER LEVEL. This phase runs from 25 feet and beyond. It is what occurs in crowded shopping areas when nonverbals are sent (even though we are usually unaware of this message being trans-mitted) to others about how we will pass them in an aisle. There is usually no transfer of words. It is not necessary to get to know the other person or spend any amount of time in the exchange.

• LECTURE LEVEL. This is a space of about 12 to 25 feet around us. Teachers maintain this level when lecturing to their classes. The listener uses visual clues — such as eyes and lips — to get the complete message. The structure of speech usually changes and is much more formal. There is not a lot of per-sonal sharing on this level.

• IMPERSONAL SPACE. This is a social space. This area is reserved for casual friends and acquain-tances, for co-workers, and for general socializing. The distance is about 4 to 12 feet. The close social space is 4 to 7 feet, while the far social space is 7 to 12 feet. The level of activity for this area is imper-sonal.

• PERSONAL SPACE. This is an individual's per-sonal zone. It extends from 18 inches to approxi-mately 4 feet in all directions. This is a space reserved for good friends and for discussing personal issues. Inside this space, friends tell each other their troubles. The sharing that occurs within this distance is of a personal nature. Three-dimensional vision is present. The person is outside of breath range. Body heat cannot usually be detected.

• CONFIDENTIAL. This is also called Intimate Space. It is closest to a person. The intimate zone extends outward from a person in all directions to approximately 18 inches. It is reserved for loved ones. It occasionally includes family members and a few close friends. At 18 inches, the physical presence of another person is overwhelming. Faces are blurred and distorted. Three-dimensional vision is lost. Breath is easily detected. Warmth from body heat is felt. The features of the other person appear monstrously large.

We also have another space that is approximately three feet around us. This is a DEFENSIVE ZONE. When one is upset, angry or frustrated, no one is welcome in this space. We have a tendency to keep people out and even to move back when another person invades this space.

Communication is a tool for survival. It is the principal means of understanding ourselves and our environment. It is a source of enjoyment and information, and is a device for problem-solving. It determines our success and happiness. Communication keeps relationships alive and well. It is essential in maintaining an organization and for its survival. Communication keeps the organization's members in touch with one another so they can work harmoniously. Without communication, societies, groups, institutions, families and relationships would cease to exist.

When you communicate, you communicate yourself. You report what happens inside of you. Sharing this information determines the quality of the relationship. The closer you are to a person, the more you open yourself to that person. You share your thoughts and feelings. You risk and become more vulnerable as you disclose who you are. You reveal your values and the things that are important to you.

Communication implies that there are at least two people in an exchange. One is the sender; the other is the listener. The sender is the "talker" (if words are being used). The sender is giving off the message. The choice of words one uses is important. The message must have a common level of understanding. It would not benefit either party if one person was speaking Russian and the other could not speak or understand that language.

Listening is a skill that takes a conscious effort on a person's part to use. We've all experienced a situation where one has not felt understood or heard. Sometimes, it feels like we're talking to a brick wall. It's hard to know if someone is paying attention and hearing our message when they are staring at a television set or reading a newspaper while we are pouring out our heart.

A listener has to observe the speaker for nonverbal clues in order to hear the whole message. Words are just part of it. One must also listen for feelings, and look at facial expressions and gestures to hear the complete message. Eye contact must be maintained. The disadvantage is that we think faster than we can talk.

According to researcher Ralph Nichols, the average person talks at a rate of 125 words per minute. If thoughts were measured in words per minute, most of us could think easily at about four times that rate. That's why we have to slow down our thinking to be a listener. That is a difficult and sometimes painful process. We have about 400 words of thinking time to spare for every minute a person talks to us.

Several factors influence how we hear. The following are not listed in any priority:

1. OUR BACKGROUND. Your past influences you and thus determines your reactions at times. Your background — where you grew up, your schooling, your family structure, the people who were in your life and so on — are all filters through which you hear messages.

2. YOUR EXPERIENCES. Trips you have made, awards you have won, competitions you've lost, love relationships, betrayal of friends, successes, failures — all of those play roles in how we listen.

3. FAMILY INFLUENCES. If you grew up in a close-knit family where openness and sharing were modeled, then you are more comfortable being open. If affection was openly displayed, you are more comfortable giving and receiving hugs. If you grew up with a lot of violence and abuse, you have been scarred by those.

4. YOU'RE OWN PERCEPTION of your physical body influences how you can be attentive to another's message. If you hold negative thoughts about your body and think you are ugly, those negative messages come through.

5. YOUR PERSONALITY STYLE. Some people are outgoing and are talkers. Some are quiet and withdrawn. Some need to be around others. Others need more alone time.

6. EDUCATION. Since words are the common

denominator in transmitting the message, our educational level influences (to some extent) our vocabulary.

7. FRIENDS. The experiences we've had with our friends stretch us and teach us how to interact with others. Acceptance and rejection teach us to cope. Friends help us learn to be who we are and challenge us to be who we truly can be. They allow us to show them our good sides and the sides of us that are not always soft and kind — and they still are our friends.

8. GOALS WE'VE SET and accomplishments we've achieved help us filter others' messages. Goals we have not accomplished also tell us something about ourselves. The way we know who we are influences how we can know anyone else.

The following are a few suggestions to use in improving your communication. The better you feel about how you communicate the happier you'll be:

• CONSCIOUSLY PAY ATTENTION to someone who is talking to you and slow your mind down to hear the whole message. Do not interrupt the speaker.

• TRY NOT TO GIVE ADVICE. No one really wants it. People just keep asking until they hear what they want to hear.

• LISTEN TO YOURSELF. Are your messages negative? If so, work hard at stopping that negative thought. If you are negative, it will teach you to listen to negativity from someone else.

• DON'T PREACH or lecture. Your opinions are only your opinions. Unless the other really asks for them, keep them to yourself.

• HAVE THE COURAGE TO SAY, "I'M SORRY." We all make mistakes. We sometimes say things too quickly. Admitting it will help hurts heal.

• KEEP YOUR SENTENCES SHORT. Sometimes, we all talk too much. People listen only to what they want to hear.

• CHOOSE TO BE ASSERTIVE. Assertiveness implies you are respectful of yourself and the other. The other options are to be submissive or aggressive. Submissiveness implies the other person must be all right, but you aren't. Submissive people can never say "no." Your body posture begins to take on the stance that you are withdrawn. Your shoulders start to droop, your head goes down, you resist eye contact, and you allow people to walk over you. You are never as important as the other.

Aggressive people have no regard for the other. The only thing that matters is that the aggressive person gets what he needs. It doesn't even matter if it is at someone else's expense. People who are aggressive yell in a loud tone of voice, finger-point, use "you messages" that remind you that it's YOUR fault, and not only keep eye contact but stare right through you.

In both the aggressive and the submissive model, someone loses. But in the assertive model, everyone can win. Assertive responses are clear, simple and direct.

• WATCH THE FACE of the other person while you are talking. Are they listening? Do they look shocked or surprised? Do they look amused or entertained?

• ASK QUESTIONS. It's a wonderful way to further a conversation and keep it focused on the other.

• BE SURE IT'S A GOOD TIME to talk to the other. If it isn't, be content to wait until it is.

• DON'T BRING UP OLD GARBAGE. To remind someone over and over again of something they did will never create an environment where communication will be open and honest. Who wants to be in the presence of someone who reminds you of your faults all the time?

• PREPARE. If you want to talk to someone about something of importance, get your facts together. Know your own feelings. Say what you want to say out loud. Look in a mirror while you're talking and watch for your own facial expressions. Choose words that the other will be able to hear and not ones filled with value-laden messages.

• IDENTIFY THE PROBLEM or issue you want to talk about. State it clearly and simply.

• BE OPEN to the other person's solutions and ideas. You may find out that the suggestion works better that any you could have thought of.

• DON'T GET SARCASTIC. Sarcasm is cloaked aggression. If you are angry, state you are angry and tell what you are angry about.

• SHARE FUNNY STORIES and joyful events. You can brighten another's day when you do.

Chapter Fourteen

—❧—

TICKLE YOUR SOUL

This chapter is not a be-all-end-all. It is meant to serve as an idea list. One person's ideas often trigger several ideas for someone else. There is no priority in these. One idea isn't better than another. This is just an attempt to add a few thoughts on how to increase joy, laughter and humor in our lives.

Some of these are suggestions. Some are little strategies. Some will bring a smile to your face. Others will present a challenge to you. Enjoy them — and then add your own ideas to the list.

Most importantly, promise yourself that you will do at least three conscious things a day that increase the joy, laughter and humor in your life.

Here's my list:

• DON'T TAKE YOURSELF SO SERIOUSLY. Make at least three mistakes a day on purpose. Anything over and above that earns bonus points. Chalk up as many as you can. To be human means to make mistakes. Celebrate that gift of being human.

• ASK FOR WHAT YOU NEED. To be able to relax

enough to see the joy in front of you, you have to realize you can't do it alone. To let others help you is a gift to them and a gift to you.

• SMILE MORE. It increases the value of your face. Also makes people want to be around you more. It may even make people wonder what you are up to.

• ENJOY THE NOW. Joy is in the present moment. Yesterday has no value. Tomorrow isn't here yet. The energy is only in this moment.

• GIVE SOMETHING AWAY every day. I'm not talking about a material possession. I'm talking about a smile. A kind word. A spontaneous phone call to someone who needs to hear from someone. A card or note sent to say you are thinking of someone.

• DECIDE TO LIVE TODAY FULLY. Don't die without ever living.

• SPEND SOME QUIET TIME. It lowers anxiety and helps with focusing. There is enough anxious activity in our culture. The very human and holy art of being able to sit still is a spiritual behavior. Psalm 45 reminds us, "Be still and know that I am God."

• LEARN TO LAUGH AT YOURSELF. If you can't laugh at yourself, you are never free to see the humor in the paradoxes that occur in our daily lives.

• GIVE YOURSELF 15 MINUTES out of each day that is your self-indulgence time. Use that time to do something that energizes your body with laughter. You can spend more time if possible, but you must spend at least 15 minutes a day.

• MAKE A LIST of twenty things that make you happy. Then make a contract with yourself to do at least three of those each day.

• LEARN TO EVALUATE SITUATIONS. What's the worst possible thing that can happen? Is it really as bad as you thought? It may mean a bit of an inconvenience or the fact that you will not have something done exactly as you had planned, but does it have to become the end of the world?

• DIFFERENTIATE BETWEEN WANTS AND NEEDS. There is a huge difference between them. If you need something, then you cannot live without it. Like oxygen, for instance. You need it to breathe. But do you really need that car? Or VCR? Or a person in your life to make you happy?

• MAKE A LIST OF THINGS THAT UPLIFT YOU. Be creative. Don't limit yourself at all. On my list would be things like a phone call from a friend, a sunset, a sunrise and receiving a compliment. Once you become aware of things that give you a sense of being uplifted, you can get mileage out of them when they happen in your life. The reality is they happen everyday. We are just not aware of them.

• BELIEVE IN SANTA CLAUS. Let the little child in you be real and alive. Giggle like a little child, too.

• PLAN AHEAD. To have fun and do things you enjoy requires that you assure yourself that you have these things in your life. That means planning on a daily basis. You are a worthwhile person, so be sure to put into your daily routine the events, people and things that tickle your soul.

- GIVE YOURSELF PERMISSION TO BE "YOU." Sometimes, we need to accept ourselves where we are right then and there. Allow yourself some breathing space. Allow yourself some time to walk slowly or to limp through your wounds until you can learn to walk and run again.

- KEEP A JOURNAL and read through it every so often. You'll surprise yourself at your own progress through your own journey.

- FIND A SUPPORT GROUP or a club that you can associate with that shares a common interest or concern. We are social beings. We need others. What a gift we give ourselves when we let others be there for us.

- FIND QUOTES or sayings or posters that are helpful to you. Display them where you can see them often. Your dresser mirror or bathroom mirror are good spots.

- DON'T WASTE YOUR TIME on people who do not want to be in your life.

- KEEP A SENSE OF BALANCE in your life: work, play, read, relax, rest and pray.

- TAKE YOUR LIFE ONE MOMENT, one second, one hour, one day at a time.

- RISK LEARNING new things and developing new interests. Take time for activities that can bring some purpose in your life.

- DON'T WASTE YOUR LIFE WITH WORRY. Deal with what is real. Worry means we're trying to control situations. But that requires a lot of energy which has no positive outcome. Decide when you will worry: when you're sitting in a specific chair...in the shower...at a designated time, like between 6:00 p.m. and 6:15 p.m. each evening.

• FOCUS ON YOUR SURROUNDINGS and find the beauty there. Let the warmth of a fireplace, the beauty of a first snowfall, or the angelic face of an elderly person touch your heart.

• LAUGH. And then laugh some more. Then laugh again. Exercise your lungs, and bring the gift of life and humor to every waking moment of your life.

• CHOOSE TO BE A HAPPY PERSON. Find the positive in any situation.

• CELEBRATE as often as you can. Birthdays, anniversaries and other significant days that hold special meanings do not need to be celebrated only once a year. Find a reason to throw a party.